Our Pets

Dogs

by Lisa J. Amstutz

raintree

a Capstone company — publishers for children

Raintree is an imprint of Capstone Global Library Limited, a company incorporated in England and Wales having its registered office at 264 Banbury Road, Oxford, OX2 7DY – Registered company number: 6695582

www.raintree.co.uk
myorders@raintree.co.uk

Edited by Marissa Kirkman
Designed by Juliette Peters (cover) and Charmaine Whitman (interior)
Picture research by Morgan Walters
Production by Laura Manthe
Originated by Capstone Global Library Limited
Printed and bound in India

ISBN 978 1 4747 5715 7
21 20 19 18 17
10 9 8 7 6 5 4 3 2 1

British Library Cataloguing in Publication Data
A full catalogue record for this book is available from the British Library.

Acknowledgements
We would like to thank the following for permission to reproduce photographs: iStockphoto: JMichl, left 9; Shutterstock: Africa Studio, 21, alexei_tm, 5, anetapics, 13, Anna Goroshnikova, 1, Anna Hoychuk, top right 9, 17, Dora Zett, back cover, frank60, 15, Grisha Bruev, bottom 11, Kateryna Mostova, 7, Mr Aesthetics, (wood) design element throughout, otsphoto, Cover, Richard Chaff, top 11, Yuriy Koronovskiy, 19

Contents

Listen!

Woof!

What is that sound?

It is a dog barking!

This barking dog is excited.

It's time for a walk!

The dog wags its tail.

All about dogs

Some dogs are big.

They can almost fill a bath.

Other dogs are tiny.

They can sit on your lap.

Look at those curls!

Dogs have all kinds of coats.

Some have long, soft hair.

Others have short, stiff hair.

Dogs have some
very good senses.
They hear sounds people can't.
Dogs can follow a scent trail.
Sniff!

Growing up

Look!

A litter of puppies is born.
They drink milk from
their mum.

Puppies grow quickly.
In four weeks, they
eat solid food.

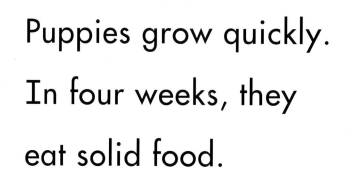

Dogs and you

Dogs love to play
with you.
They can go and get a ball.
Fetch!

Dogs are great friends.

They are loyal.

Dogs are happy just to
be with you!

Glossary

coat animal's hair or fur

fetch to go after something and bring it back; some dogs will fetch a ball or a toy

litter group of animals born at the same time to the same mother

loyal being true to something or someone

puppy young dog

scent smell

sense way of knowing about your surroundings; hearing, smelling, touching, tasting and sight are senses

sniff to breathe in quickly through the nose

wag to move from side to side; dogs wag their tails when they are happy

Read more

Caring for Dogs and Puppies (Battersea Dogs and Cats Home: Pet Care Guides), Ben Hubbard (Franklin Watts, 2015)

Dogs: Questions and Answers (Pet Questions and Answers), Christina Mia Gardeski (Capstone Press, 2017)

Ruff's Guide to Caring for Your Dog (Pets' Guides), Anita Ganeri (Raintree, 2014)

Websites

www.bbc.co.uk/cbeebies/topics/pets
Discover a variety of pets, play pet games and watch pet videos on this fun BBC website.

www.bluecross.org.uk
Find out more about how to choose a pet and care for your pet on the Blue Cross website.

Comprehension questions

1. Would you like to own a dog? Why or why not?

2. What do newborn puppies eat?

3. Why do dogs make good pets?

Index